## ADRIANA LUNA CARLOS

Editor-In-Chief, Designer and
Co-Founder

## HANNA OLIVAS

Managing Editor & Co-Founder

# SUCCESS
# SAVVY

**ADVERTISING
OPPORTUNITIES**
Info@SheRisesStudios.com

**CONTACT US**
SheRisesStudios@gmail.com
www.SheRisesStudios.com

**SUCCESS SAVVY** MAY 2024

**SHE RISES**
S T U D I O S

www.SheRisesStudios.com

# LETTER FROM THE EDITORS

Dear Readers,

As we dive into the vibrant pages of the May 2024 issue, Success Savvy Magazine it is with immense excitement and pride that I introduce you to a trailblazer who is reshaping the industry of beauty, lifestyle, and digital innovation in the 21st century—Shalini Vadhera. Her captivating journey, eloquently chronicled in the featured article titled "Redefining Beauty, Lifestyle, and Digital Innovation in the 21st Century," invites us into a world where innovation, empowerment, and global impact converge.

Shalini Vadhera, a visionary entrepreneur with a background that spans jewelry, fashion, and now a multi-million dollar global cosmetics empire, has seamlessly embraced the digital era to push boundaries and challenge norms. Her story is not just about business success; it's a narrative of empowerment, community building, and a commitment to positive change on a global scale.

In "Redefining Beauty, Lifestyle, and Digital Innovation in the 21st Century," Shalini shares insights into her ventures, from the inception of Ready Set Jet—a brand dedicated to on-the-go innovation and community impact—to the global influence of The Power Beauty Living Foundation. Her journey underscores the transformative power of digital media in spreading her mission of empowering confident women worldwide.

Shalini's Passport To Beauty brand, which brings the world's best beauty secrets to consumers, takes center stage as we explore how digital content has become an integral part of connecting with a diverse audience. The article unveils how the digital age has played a pivotal role in Shalini's success, from launching products in renowned retailers to shaping the narrative and perception of her brands.

As you immerse yourselves in Shalini's remarkable story, you'll witness the fusion of innovative formulations, unique packaging design, and global recognition. The digital era not only amplifies her philanthropic efforts but also invites readers into the creative process, where real-time feedback shapes the evolution of her products.
\
Shalini Vadhera, with her numerous accolades and recognition, stands as an inspiration for aspiring entrepreneurs, especially women, navigating the beauty and lifestyle industry. Her advice resonates with passion, perseverance, and the endless possibilities that digital innovation presents in today's interconnected world.

We invite you to embark on this journey with us—exploring the intersection of beauty, lifestyle, and digital innovation through the lens of Shalini Vadhera's visionary perspective. May you be inspired by her accomplishments, motivated by her words, and empowered to embrace your unique vision in this ever-evolving digital age.

Here's to redefining beauty, lifestyle, and digital innovation in the 21st century!

Warm regards,

Adriana Luna Carlos and Hanna Olivas
Editors of Success Savvy Magazine

# WOMEN ON THE
*Rise*

# REDEFINING BEAUTY, LIFESTYLE, AND DIGITAL INNOVATION IN THE 21ST CENTURY

## *SHALINI VADHERA*

Shalini Vadhera, the visionary entrepreneur who seamlessly transitioned from the work of jewelry and fashion to revolutionize the beauty industry, has become a trailblazer in the digital age. Her journey is an inspiring testament to the boundless opportunities that arise at the intersection of beauty, lifestyle, and digital innovation.

### Empowering Confidence Worldwide

As the founder of Ready Set Jet, a brand committed to innovative on-the-go products and community impact, Shalini envisions the role of digital media as a catalyst for spreading the mission of empowering confident women globally. Through a groundbreaking crowdfunding campaign, the brand democratized investment, allowing women worldwide to own equity for as little as $100. Social media platforms were harnessed to disrupt traditional investment paradigms, fostering a global community of ambassadors and advocates for the brand.

### Global Impact through The Power Beauty Living Foundation

Shalini's remarkable accomplishment of launching The Power Beauty Living Foundation at the United Nations in 2016 stands as a testament to her commitment to global empowerment. Digital innovation played a pivotal role in expanding the foundation's reach and impact, enabling a mix of online and offline mentorship and training programs. The foundation's global mission to empower women, irrespective of socio-economic status, was amplified through digital platforms, creating a far-reaching impact.

### Passport To Beauty: Connecting Diverse Audiences

Passport To Beauty, Shalini's beauty brand, leverages the age of digital content to bring the world's best beauty secrets to consumers worldwide. By collaborating with a digital content studio, Shalini took her audience on a journey, sharing behind-the-scenes content of product development. This immersive approach not only showcased beauty diversity but also connected with a diverse audience, providing a unique and personal experience to consumers around the globe.

### Digital Strategies Driving Retail Success

Placing over $100 million in products across renowned retailers like Sephora, QVC, Victoria's Secret, and HSN is a testament to Shalini's mastery of digital strategies. Utilizing digital advertising, influencer partnerships, affiliate collaborations, and data-driven marketing, Shalini maximized brand visibility and community engagement, paving the way for her products to thrive in these prominent retail spaces.

### Amplifying Empowerment and Philanthropy

Shalini's recognition with prestigious awards reflects her outstanding contributions to empowerment and philanthropy. Through digital media, she amplifies her message, inspiring action and mobilizing global support. Experiential events, such as Ayurvedic cocktail parties and workshops, facilitated by digital media, bring together a community of empowered women who drive positive change on a global scale.

### Shaping Narratives in the Digital Age

Being a go-to brand innovator for Hollywood studios, celebrities, and influencers, Shalini has strategically used digital media to shape the narrative and perception of Passport To Beauty and Ready Set Jet. By sharing authentic stories through engaging content and meaningful in-person experiences, Shalini has fostered strong relationships built on trust, authenticity, and a shared commitment to women empowerment.

### The Creative Process Unveiled Online

Shalini's focus on innovative formulations and unique packaging design has garnered global recognition. In the digital era, she utilizes online platforms to showcase the creative process behind her products, inviting real-time feedback and co-creating with her audience. This crowd-sourcing approach not only adds transparency to the creative process but also builds a sense of community among consumers.

### Extending TV Appearances through Digital Engagement

As a favorite guest on renowned shows, Shalini extends the reach of her appearances through digital media. Deeper blog posts, live engagements, and a strong social media presence enable her to connect with a broader audience interested in beauty and lifestyle content. This multifaceted approach transcends traditional TV audiences, creating lasting relationships with viewers around the world.

### Words of Wisdom for Aspiring Entrepreneurs

Shalini Vadhera shares her advice for aspiring entrepreneurs, especially women, in the beauty and lifestyle industry. Embrace your unique vision, stay true to your values, and leverage the power of the digital world. In today's age, where possibilities are endless, passion, perseverance, and a willingness to adapt can help aspiring entrepreneurs make their mark and inspire positive change in the world. Shalini Vadhera's journey exemplifies the transformative impact of embracing the intersection of beauty, lifestyle, and digital innovation in the 21st century.

www.instagram.com/shalinivadhera | www.facebook.com/shalinisworld | www.linktr.ee/shalinivadhera

# BEYOND LIMITS: HOW TO DISMANTLE SELF-IMPOSED BOUNDARIES AND THRIVE

By: Sally Pederson

As I opened the basement door, I fell to my knees; I knew my life would never be the same after what I saw. In a world where the only constant is change, the journey of personal transformation often begins at the edge of our comfort zone. Massive change happens when something happens to you or within you. In this space, beyond the familiar boundaries we set for ourselves, true growth occurs.

Like many others, my story is a testament to the resilience of the human spirit in the face of loss and adversity. It began with the painful closure of a chapter in my life, marked by the court-ordered death certificate of my missing husband, confirming his murder. The compounded grief of losing a long-term relationship and the sudden death of another partner from an aneurysm plunged me into profound sorrow. These moments of darkness, however, became the catalysts for a profound personal transformation.

Faced with the depths of despair, I stood at a crossroads. The path forward was not illuminated by the light of certainty but by the glimmer of hope and the yearning for change. Then, I faced a moral dilemma that tested my values to their core. A lucrative but compromising proposal from a business partner threatened to sway me from my principles. The choice was clear yet daunting: embrace my integrity or succumb to the allure of comfort and security.

Choosing integrity, I turned my back on what was familiar and embarked on a journey to Costa Rica, seeking a fresh start. This decision was met with resistance and concern, especially from my teenage daughter, who struggled to adapt to our new life. Yet, this move was more than a change of scenery; it was a profound leap of faith into the unknown, driven by a belief in the possibility of a life aligned with my deepest values and aspirations.

TThe first step in dismantling self-imposed boundaries is embracing your authentic self. My journey taught me the importance of staying true to my values, even when faced with tempting alternatives. Authenticity is the compass that guides us through life's challenges and decisions, ensuring we remain aligned with our true north.

Resilience is not merely the ability to bounce back from adversity; it's the capacity to transform pain into a stepping stone for growth. Each loss, each setback, has the potential to teach us invaluable lessons about ourselves and the world around us. Embracing resilience means viewing every challenge as an opportunity to learn and evolve.

Change requires courage—the courage to let go of the familiar, to face the unknown, and to take risks. My move to Costa Rica symbolized a leap into uncertainty, driven by the conviction that there was more to life than the limitations I had previously accepted. It's in the moments of decision that our destiny is shaped.

No journey is undertaken alone. The support of friends, family, and mentors is invaluable as we navigate the challenges of change. Their encouragement, advice, and presence provide the strength and perspective to persevere when the path becomes arduous.

Today, as I reflect on the journey that led me beyond the limits, I once imposed on myself, I am grateful for the lessons learned and the growth experienced. The decision to dismantle those boundaries and embrace the uncertainty of change has led to a more prosperous, more fulfilling life. It's a testament to the fact that when we dare to step beyond our self-imposed limits, we open ourselves to the infinite possibilities life offers.

To anyone standing at the edge of their comfort zone, contemplating the leap into the unknown, know that a world of potential is waiting to be discovered beyond the fear and uncertainty. The boundaries we perceive are often of our own making, and it's within our power to dismantle them. Let my story be a reminder that it's never too late to redefine your path, embrace change, and thrive beyond limits.

# CREATING CONFIDENCE TO UNLEASH THE POWERFUL WOMAN

## Trish Gleason

Have you ever gorged down a donut after someone gave you a compliment? This is a stepping stone to building & keeping confidence. Create stepping stones to build your self-esteem.

Your confidence constantly needs replenishment, especially today in a society where bullying, judgements & criticism is the norm. We receive NATURAL stepping stones such as compliments about our hairstyle or successes. A new professional license is an example of a self-created stepping stone and although you may not receive accolades, internally you are proud of improving your confidence. Let's delve into what women are up against.

"According to a study in 2023 by the National Bureau of Economic Research, close to 80% of women struggle with low self-esteem and shy away from self-advocacy at work". One study shows 78% of girls age 17 are unhappy with their bodies creating a lifelong self-esteem battle.

Most people would define me as very confident - but it wasn't always like that. I was very insecure with low self esteem during my entire elementary school years. I never raised my hand even once. My 3rd grade teacher mocked me in the front of the class creating a valuable lesson. I was petrified to speak in front of the class so when the teacher called my name I put both hands/fingers to my mouth and began chomping away biting my fingernails, as usual. When I did not answer, the teacher put her fingers in her mouth & began moving them back & forth like she was eating corn on the cob on steroids mocking me. This was a bona-fide CHOP DOWN and I soon realized people were going to do this for the rest of my life. I had to recover by building my self-esteem back up. When someone chops me down now I have learned to rebuild myself, to rebuild my confidence back to the same or better.

3 easy ways to purposely create new or natural STEPPING STONES to build your confidence in a fast track way.

1. Affirmations - Look in the mirror every day and give yourself the best of compliments. Tell yourself you are successful, be positive. Have you heard of phone telemarketers keeping a mirror at their desk to make sure they are smiling all the time? It's true, it works. Search google about affirmations to learn many lessons.
2. Smiling - This activates sensors in your brain to trick you into happiness and boost your health. Dr. I. Gupta, a neurologist from IGEA Brain and Spine explains, "a smile spurs a chemical reaction in the brain, releasing certain hormones including dopamine and serotonin to increase our feelings of happiness. Serotonin is associated with reduced stress. Low levels of serotonin are associated with depression and aggression."
3. Create your own stepping stones or put yourself in a position to receive and recognize natural stepping stones. Dressing up, being purposeful in your attire and good attitude and attending events to create a stepping stone. Put yourself in a position to get a natural complement. If you're a great baker, create something grand and take it to an event to "fish" for a compliment. We all need to build up our confidence.

Go to www.theworldwellnessshow.com to learn holistic education from world renown doctors on FENIXtv.app - broadcasting in 137 countries. Help others by giving them compliments to help them with their stepping stones in life and discourage any attempts to inadvertently "chop down" anyone. Be purposeful knowing you need to rebuild your confidence and self-esteem every day.

**THE WORLD WELLNESS**
Show
est. 2018

# GAGAN SODHI

## Trading Places:
## Culture Shock Ignites
## Entrepreneurial Spark

Over the past few decades, women have made massive strides in financial independence. More women are starting their own businesses. More women are managing the fine balance of working and caring responsibilities.

Women are making their mark in industries typically dominated by men. One of those industries is trading. Women are challenging entrenched norms and reshaping industries historically dominated by men. These disruptors are changing the status quo and leading the way. I never thought I'd be a disrupter.

Originally from a traditional Indian household where the role of a woman is clearly defined, the move with my husband to Australia in 2006 sparked a shift, from the comforts of a home with servants to the unfamiliarity of handling household chores in a new country; it marked a profound cultural shock. Despite my family's roots in India, where norms suggested that as a woman, I need not work, my aspirations reached beyond the expected roles of studying, obtaining a degree, marrying, and raising a family.

Transitioning from a household with servants to personally tackling chores was a culture shock that defined our early days in the land down under.

Australia, with its stark differences from my Indian upbringing, became a challenge and opportunity. Without the familiar embrace of family, the cultural shock reverberated as we compared our lives in Australia to the comforts of our parents' homes in India. Paying money to the government, managing our household chores, and even washing dishes became bewildering tasks in this new reality.

The juxtaposition of studying alongside household duties created an overwhelming situation, prompting me to question my role and purpose. The initial carefree living in a rented house masked the reality that funds would eventually run out.

As financial constraints tightened their grip, I considered drastic measures, like pawning a cherished bracelet to make ends meet. The urgency of the situation hit home when the pawn shop owner warned me he would keep it if not retrieved by evening. Thankfully, I managed to gather the necessary funds in the nick of time.

I knew I wanted to do something with the skills, education and opportunities that came from changing our lives. After many years of trading and learning all I could about trading, I was often the only woman in the room. I immersed myself in learning all I could, and kept seeing people make the same mistakes over and over, impacting their trading journey.

Driven by an insatiable thirst for knowledge, I invested nearly $50k in studying Forex and trading. Engaging in courses facilitated by notable figures such as Greg Seckor, Timothy Sykes, ICT, and Raja Banks, I witnessed firsthand the struggles of traders losing hard-earned money.

This experience, coupled with industry experts' calls for robust risk management tools, catalysed my decision to take action. I offer traders a haven to rewind time and practice live historical data, including news events. This project is a guardian angel for traders, providing a valuable risk management tool to minimise overtrading and excessive risk-taking.

The genesis of MT5 Trade Ready sprang from my personal struggles with overtrading and risk management in the trading arena. With a dearth of products addressing these concerns, I wanted to create a solution. What ensued was a rigorous six-month journey involving over 100 iterations to develop the initial version of the software.

At its core, MT5 Trade Ready serves as a risk management tool, designed to limit users to a specified number of trades per day, making it highly customizable. The software disrupts the prevalent culture of overtrading and financial loss in the industry. It's a safety mechanism, like red lights on roads, intended to mitigate risky behaviour.

By helping traders manage their risk, I also see the platform having positive ripple effects, extending beyond traders' finances to encompass family dynamics and well-being.

 https://gagansodhiofficial.com/
 Gagan.Sodhi.Official/

# 5 proven steps to help you find your dream career.

## by: Kristy Weterings

**Step 1: Get to know Yourself.**

When you don't know who you are, what gives you energy and what skills and talents you're naturally good at, you are like a ship that has set sail with no direction. We have been formed and shaped into the person we are today by our upbringing, where we lived, our friends, our hobbies, etc. Through this we have acquired certain skills that we might have become good at but that don't necessarily give us energy or make us happy. We end up choosing a job that doesn't make us happy but that's approved by society, that gives us security, status, and a good paycheck. What eventually happens is that we hop from one job to the next, hoping that the next one will be more fulfilling, only to discover that none of them keep us feeling fulfilled. So, my advice to you is before you start scrolling endlessly on LinkedIn looking for a new job, go on an inner journey first, discover who you truly are, what gives you energy, and what will make you happy in a job.

**Step 2: Master your Mindset.**

Women usually stay in an unfulfilling job because their fears, self-doubt and limiting beliefs are standing in the way of what they want. Remember that these are just beliefs, they are not the truth. You need to stop letting this negative voice inside your head (which is just trying to keep you safe and in your comfort zone) take control over your life. From this position, you will only search for jobs that suit the image of what others expect from you, leaving you feeling unhappy. Therefore, it's vital that you start working on your mindset and start shifting your beliefs to more positive ones.

**Step 3: Dream Big.**

Imagine if anything is possible, what would you do? Imagine if you had all time, money, and skills that you need to realize your dream, what would you do? When we were children, we had huge fantasies and could make up all sorts of fantasy stories. As we get older our fantasy gets less triggered and we forget how to just let our thoughts run wild. Your brain will always try and keep you safe. Your brain is developed in such a way that it will focus on the negative and keep you in your comfort zone because it wants to protect you from pain and danger.

Your brain would rather want you to be unhappy and safe than out of your comfort zone and happy. Instead of listening to the negative voices inside your head try to let your creative brain go. Imaging if anything is possible, what would you do?

**Step 4: Get clear on your why.**

Try to imagine your future self. Who do you want to be? How do you want to feel? What do you want your future life to look like if you could have anything and do anything you want? When you are not crystal clear on why you want to change your career, you will never get into action towards achieving your goals and dreams. When you know the bigger picture of why you want to do a certain thing you will be more motivated and driven to achieve that goal. Then you know what kind of impact it will eventually make on those around you. Step 5: Take action. We tend to procrastinate because we want everything to be perfect. Perfectionism will prevent you from taking action. If you wait for all the circumstances to be perfect before you decide to make a change, you will be waiting for a very long time.

**Step 5: Take action.**

We tend to procrastinate because we want everything to be perfect. Perfectionism will prevent you from taking action. If you wait for all the circumstances to be perfect before you decide to make a change, you will be waiting for a very long time.

Many women don't take action because they have so many ideas that they can't choose. They are also afraid of making the wrong choice and feel like they are not ready. Remember, you can always change your course along the way if you need to. Even if it's a tiny step in the right direction. You don't have to see the whole staircase, just take the first step.

What small action step can you take today?

Website: https://kristyweterings.com/
Instagram: https://www.instagram.com/kristy_weterings/

# WOMEN IN
# BU$INESS

# FINDING LIGHT THROUGH LOSS:
## A JOURNEY OF LOVE, GRIEF, AND RESILIENCE

by: Nicole Kolb

**Do you find yourself asking, 'Will I ever just feel better again?'** I know that question all too well. After losing my identical twin girls, Storm, my stillborn, and her sister Logan, who survived just two and a half days, my world shattered. It was a stark contrast... life and death, rage and love, despair and hope. What happened next was my own personal hell, and I was determined to find my way out.

On January 10, 2019, I became a first-time mom; by January 13, I had no children. In the following months, while searching for answers, I became pregnant with my healthy baby boy, Rogan, and 10 months later, a single mom. The shock and trauma consumed me for years, leaving me feeling frozen in a living hell, yet every morning, I mustered the courage to face another day.

I never thought I'd find peace, love, and laughter again, but I did, and it's available for you too. Healing from such immeasurable loss takes time, community, and courage. For me, courage meant getting out of bed each day, even when I wanted time to stop.

If my words resonate with you, I'm deeply sorry for your loss. And please know, healing is possible. The first step is giving yourself time to process what happened. If I could start over, I'd allow myself more grace, more time to just be, cry, and scream, understanding that no feeling is final.

Unconditional love first became real to me in the NICU, holding my daughter Logan's tiny foot. Surrounded by tubes and the beeps of machines, I whispered, 'You got this, my baby. Keep fighting.' This moment was a turning point, teaching me about unconditional love and the beginning of my journey into self-love. Months later, as tears streamed down my face in front of my bathroom mirror, I realised that if I could create something so perfect, I must be perfect too. It started with a simple phrase, 'I am lovable,' repeated until it finally took root.

Truthfully, I never wanted children initially, but life had other plans. My pregnancy with Rogan, born from trauma, didn't allow me the joy I had heard about. Becoming a single mom added to the overwhelming challenge. I had to dig deep, finding strength and compassion within myself, to be the pillar my son needed.

A turning point in my journey came with the tragic loss of my magical friend, who, unable to bear the pain of her own baby loss, chose to end her life. This heartbreaking event gave me a deeper understanding of the profound effects of such grief and reinforced my commitment to supporting others through their darkest times.

This realisation led to another distressing thought – what if I lost Rogan too? This fear made me recognise the need for a purpose beyond my child. I had to find something greater, echoing those who say, 'find a purpose bigger than yourself.' That's why I'm sharing my story – to discover my true purpose and help others navigate their journey through baby loss.

Healing from the loss of a baby is a path paved with courage, self-discovery, and unconditional love. It's about understanding that grief is not a linear process, and it's okay to seek help – through therapy, support groups, or simply by connecting with others who understand your pain.

If you're walking this difficult path, remember that you're not alone. You are stronger than you know, and with time, community, and self-love, you can find peace and joy again. Your journey of healing is an inward one, you have the power to save your own life.

**To connect with me and learn more about my journey, visit www.thenicolekolb.com. Together, we can walk this path of healing and rediscover our own inner strength.**

# 3 Things to Consider if you are Reaching Retirement Age

*Claribel Coreano*

We all look forward to making changes in different areas of our lives, whether it is in our careers, health or in our personal lives. Most times we are not sure what these areas look like for us. And it will require a thorough introspection of yourself, your career, and your life.

First you must start by asking yourself some difficult and challenging questions. These questions will incite your critical thinking. Ask yourself "where am I, in my personal life?" "What do I need to change?" and "How can I improve?" What is working in my life right now and what is not working for me? You may have contemplated making changes in the past, but somehow never got the courage to take the first step. You are now in a space to do something about it. You reach a point where you see it causing barriers or stagnation and showing no growth. It's time to decide, what can I do to change this situation around?

The good thing is that we can always do some things to enhance our personal life, whether it is taking the initiative to take better care of yourself or doing something for yourself that will bring you peace, calm or improve your health & wellbeing. Think about what are 3 areas of your life that you feel that you can improve? Then think about ways that you can start to work on achieving these goals.

The same when evaluating your career, you reach a stage where you are finding yourself that you are no longer growing, or you feel that there is no more room for you to grow in the company. You may need to ask yourself; do I allow myself to stay stagnant and wait till retirement? Or do I seek a more self-fulfilling position in the interim, until it is time for me to retire?

You must evaluate if being happy while you wait outweighs more than just holding onto a job in which you are no longer happy. It's time to reinvent yourself to a better version of you. By taking the opportunity to reflect on all the skills that you have and how they transfer into the job market. Set yourself a goal and write it down. If it requires seeking another job, start by building a list of all your accomplishments, promotions and opportunities that can increase your marketability. Then transpose it into your new resume. Make sure that you are creating a resume format that is easy to upload, concise and that relates to the position you are applying for.

Now think of what would you need to make a shift in your career? You are now reaching your retirement year. How do you plan to prepare yourself for these changes? If you are getting close to your retirement age, or you have started planning your exit. I encourage you to leave things for the next person who will be in your position. You have been there for a while, so, you can start by creating an informal manual of your responsibilities, tasks, and procedures. You want to leave an easy-to-follow cheat sheet for the next person who will do your job. Now, if you are thinking about going back to the workforce after retirement, think about what career or job will make you happy.

Here are some things to consider before leaving the job, think of creative ways to supplement your income or start a business from home. If you are thinking about starting a business, start researching or connecting yourself with the small business administration or other networking businesses agencies. Research on ways others have created businesses after retirement that have been financially successful. Think of the wisdom you have gained through the years, the skills that you have and what you bring to the table, that you make you happy, that can create an income base for you. Then write your plan on paper. The next step is to network with other similar businesses, mentors or coaches that can guide you in reaching your goals.

www.empowerglobalcoaching.com • facebook: fb/claribel.coreano

# Unveiling the Veil: Breaking the Silence on Women's Mental Health

**Kehinde Ladipo**

In modern society, women face mental health issues that don't get enough attention. Women face a plethora of difficulties that transcend both biological and cultural norms. Regretfully, these difficulties are frequently downplayed and do not receive the attention they merit. But now is the moment to investigate and evaluate women's mental wellness.

Women are frequently pressured to live up to the standards of perfection and beauty set by society. By displaying pictures of perfect models and celebrities, society sets challenging standards that many find difficult to meet. One of the main problems that women face is this. Their mental health has severely collapsed as a result of their inconsiderate quest for social acceptability, which has left them feeling awful about themselves.

Hence, women have typically been given the task of caring for the family's children, elderly, and ill members. Women therefore frequently multitask, which frequently results in tension and mental tiredness. They don't usually complain about this, but they must learn to pay more attention to their mental health and get help when needed. Hormonal fluctuations occur during menopause, puberty, and pregnancy.

The current state of mental health disorders in women can be significantly impacted by or made worse by anxiety and mood swings brought on by changes in hormone levels. This is just one more important issue affecting a woman's emotional well-being. Women must recognize the role hormones play in their mental health, understand their existence, and seek help when necessary.

Additionally, women are more likely to experience trauma and violence, including domestic abuse, sexual assault, and harassment. The aftermath of trauma can manifest in various forms, such as post-traumatic stress disorder (PTSD), depression, and substance abuse.

Breaking the silence surrounding these experiences is crucial for healing and recovery, empowering survivors to seek help and support without shame or stigma. Moreover, another disorder that may be dangerous for women is post-traumatic stress disorder (PTSD). Women may experience long-lasting effects from trauma related to assault, harassment, drug misuse, and domestic violence. Finding the bravery to share any of these stories is a first step toward recovery. It is important to empower survivors and provide assistance to them without stigmatising them.

Women frequently hesitate to ask for the aid they need when they do because they perceive men as stigmatising them. Because of obvious societal expectations that push and demand women to be strong enough to endure problems and thereby die in silence and remain unwilling to confess their issues, women tend to hold back from sharing their feelings and experiences with the public.

In recent years, there has been a growing movement to destigmatize mental health and promote openness and acceptance. Women are speaking out about their experiences, sharing their stories, and advocating for greater awareness and support. Social media platforms have become powerful tools for connecting women and fostering a sense of community, offering solidarity and encouragement in times of need.

Moreover, there has been an increasing recognition of the importance of holistic approaches to mental health, incorporating lifestyle factors such as diet, exercise, sleep, and mindfulness practices. Women are embracing self-care rituals, prioritizing their well-being, and seeking out alternative therapies and healing modalities to complement traditional treatments. A comprehensive approach to mitigating the challenges of mental health in women is gradually enjoying recognition in society. Cautious lifestyle routines aimed in this direction demand a balance of direct consumption, exercise, sleep and. Apart from traditional approaches to seeking treatment and healing modalities, women are embracing self-care rituals and prioritizing their well-being by

It's also crucial for healthcare providers to adopt a gender-sensitive approach to mental health care, recognizing the unique needs and experiences of women. Culturally competent and trauma-informed care can help bridge the gap and ensure that women receive appropriate and effective support.

The intricacy of women's mental health has made it imperative that it be given priority. By actively communicating their struggles, victims can reduce the stigma attached to mental health issues. The moment has come to end the stigma and eliminate the threat to women's mental health so that women's independence and empowerment can take center stage.

 https://www.facebook.com/ladipo.kenny

# Dawn Gaden

## From the Mud of Self-Doubt to Manifesting the Life of My Dreams

I realized my calling early in life to help people live more vibrant lives. Maybe it was the codependent mother/daughter relationship, or growing up in a family of addiction. Seeing first hand the soul sucking existence of dreams unfulfilled, drove me to find answers to why people simply exist rather than live vibrant lives. Overcoming anxiety and panic attacks, I completed graduate school, created a family, and started my own business.

This journey was not devoid of turbulence. Miscarriages, job loss, depression and cancer were just part of the journey. Like the lotus flower, my transformation came from the mud. When I was ready to rise, I learned how to calm the chaos in my mind, open my heart, and consciously create my life.

We don't always know when we're ready to show up for ourselves. We aren't always aware of when the veil of self doubt and uncertainty will be lifted. But if we continue the path of awareness, self evolution, we will continue to receive glimpses of insight, a path unfold, and then it is up to us to take the first step. It's like the lotus flower that blooms from the mud. Keep moving through, reaching for the light, you will get there. You will see clearly, and oh, you will shine so bright!

*During my journey through the mud of self discovery, I created I.V.E.A.,* a guide to tune into your deepest desires and amplify your energy for more joy, abundance and ease in your life. This is the foundation of The Image ShiftCoaching Program - a 7 month transformation through the chakras and creating a powerful positive self image. I invite you to take a look at each practice and begin to use them as a form of 'movement' through whatever mud you may find yourself in.

I ~ Intuition is your loyal guide. You have an inner compass leading you to serve and live in the energy of love and abundance. Pay attention and listen for its guidance.

V ~ Visualize with your mind's eye, and get a clear image of what your soul desires. Hold the image in your mind as your truth.

E ~ Emotions fuel your vision with love, joy, and enthusiasm as if it is already done. Feelings come first, action follows. Fuel everything you think and do with positive emotions.

A ~ Action that is inspired is required! Action from a state of chaos, overwhelm or fear only breeds more of the same. Take steps from a state that you want to create.

We are spiritual, emotional, mental, and physical beings. The body is the vehicle for the mind, and the mind is fueled by our spiritual guidance and emotional vibration. Vibrant living is aligning with the frequencies of joy, abundance and happiness. It's important to remember that we are also here to have fun!

The following is an excerpt from my YES! YES! Journal ~ 33 days at a time to get into alignment with your best self. I encourage you to give it a try. In your journal, complete these statements every day:

#1 Yes! to your desires: I am so happy and grateful now that...(say yes to your desires and dreams, and remember to dream big. Make this fun. Here is an example of how to write your #1 yes to your desire: I am so happy and grateful now that I Travel the world and serve in the bes way possible)

#2 Yes! to what inspired action I will take today: Daily action is required in order to create the life that you desire. Small steps, big steps, it doesn't matter! Every day take a step in the direction of your dreams and have fun! Remember to fuel it with high vibes - this will keep you connected to your vision!

www.createconsciousliving.com/ • www.instagram.com/dawngaden/ • www.facebook.com/dawn.gaden.3

# The SHE RISES STUDIOS PODCAST

The She Rises Studios podcast is dedicated to empowering women like you to reach their full potential and live their best lives. With inspiring stories, insightful interviews, and practical advice from experts in different industries, our podcast is your go-to source for information, inspiration, and motivation. Join us as we explore topics like:

- Overcoming self-doubt and limiting beliefs
- Building and running a successful business
- Building confidence and Self-esteem
- Navigating career transitions
- Starting and growing a business
- Balancing work and family life
- Improving physical and mental health
- Finding meaning and purpose in life
- So many more

Our guests include successful entrepreneurs, inspiring thought leaders, and everyday women who have overcome challenges and achieved their dreams. Each episode is packed with actionable tips and strategies to help you take your life to the next level.

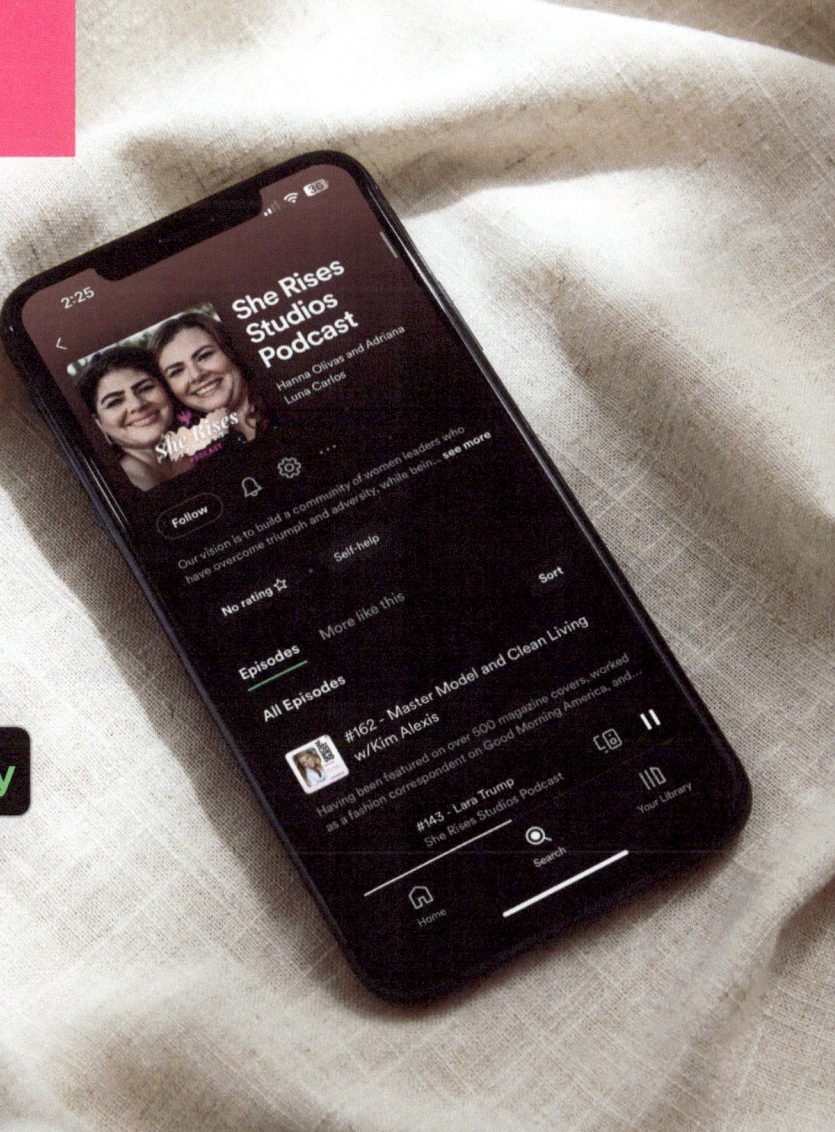

# Chantel Booley

## "Mirror, mirror, on the wall, who is the fairest of them all"

How often, as women we look in the mirror and never see the fairest of them all? We say the mirror never lies. The mirror doesn't lie but we lie to the mirror.

Women look into the mirror and tell themselves how they don't look, how they don't feel and what they see they are not. These words whether spoken out loud or silently affects our mental and emotional health.

Our minds are a great source of health to our bodies but our mental words affects our whole being.

What are you saying to yourself today?
What we tell ourselves is often what we become. Words like "you're not as young as you used to be", "who is going to love you now?", "you can't do that", "you're not good enough" and more changes the way we see ourselves and view the world around us. It also makes us think that's how others see and accept us.

How sad to think we reduce our worth ourselves more than others. Change your view of you by changing the words you use to more positive and honest ones like "you are worth more than you believe", "you can do anything you are willing to work for", "accept yourself before anyone else does" and more.

Believe me, when you change what you are telling yourself, you will feel treasured, you will walk with confidence and enjoy your life more. The world around you will see this too and love having you in their space too.

What if others put me down with their words? Forgive them and leave them behind. Women don't realize it how often we judge each other to make us feel better about ourselves. However, it actually makes us judge ourselves more and in turn, damage our own mental health. Don't be average and judge, be extraordinary and uplift!

Our time on earth and in this life is so short. Why do we waste it on creating more negativity and anxiety? The world is already in dire straits. Imagine if each woman every day embraces their image in the mirror and encourages the next woman to do the same, how the world would change.

Women, realise that you are a powerful being on this earth, and all people around you, need our nurturing and talents to uplift and create a better tomorrow.

Women, to become a super power on earth, you have to become your own super power for you.

How do you do this? Check in with yourself on a regular basis. Tell yourself all the good things that form your being, the good things you have to offer to others and the good things you still want to learn.

Not sure what the good things are? Don't be afraid to ask others what qualities they appreciate and love about you. We don't see what others see. Change your perspective on yourself and you will change your perspective of others.

Super Queen, your cape might not always be seen but let it flow behind you for you! Your power is in your mind, your emotion within your soul and your actions within your being.

Your will, your weapon!

- **www.facebook.com/simplythere**
- **www.tiktok.com/simplytherecoaching**

# KOREN NORTON

## Beyond Limits: harnessing the power of obsession to reach goals

In a world often hesitant to celebrate obsession, it's time to redefine this powerful force, recognizing it as a lighthouse guiding women toward their goals, fueling their drive, and propelling them beyond obstacles. Contrary to the negative connotations, obsession, when harnessed positively, can become the secret magic sauce that helps women to achieve unparalleled determination and success.

Obsession, at its core, is an unwavering dedication to a goal or pursuit. It's the heartbeat of passion that pulses through our veins, urging us to defy the odds and reach new heights. Women who harness this intensity, channel their energy into purposeful actions, transforming their dreams from mere possibilities into tangible realities.

Consider the woman determined to shatter the glass ceiling in her career. She doesn't just work; she obsessively strives for excellence, going above and beyond. This level of commitment often breeds innovation, setting her apart and proving that obsession, when guided by purpose, can be a formidable ally.

Obstacles are inevitable on any journey, yet it's the obsession to succeed that can help to turn roadblocks into stepping stones. Picture a budding entrepreneur launching her own business. She encounters setbacks, financial challenges, and moments of self-doubt, but her positive obsession propels her forward. Every stumble becomes a lesson, every challenge an opportunity to refine her approach.

Women who embrace positive obsession understand that challenges are not the end of the road, but an invitation to be innovative and creative. Take the artist passionately immersed in her craft. She obsessively refines her technique, views criticism as constructive feedback, and transforms challenges into triumphs. In the world of positive obsession, failure is not an endpoint but a stepping stone toward mastery.

This transformative mindset shifts the narrative around challenges. Instead of fearing them, women wielding positive obsession view obstacles as gateways to growth, resilience, and ultimately, success.

It's the ability to dance with challenges rather than be paralyzed by them that sets these women apart. Positive obsession and confidence are inseparable companions. When a woman becomes consumed by a goal, an unspoken self-assuredness emanates from within. Picture the woman entering a male-dominated field – her positive obsession with success fuels a confidence that radiates, challenging stereotypes and asserting her place at the table.

In a society that sometimes doubts or underestimates women, positive obsession becomes a force field of self-confidence. It's the belief that one's goals are not only attainable but also worth the pursuit. This intersection of obsession and confidence transforms women into trailblazers, breaking barriers and redefining what's possible.

While embracing positive obsession, it's crucial to maintain a delicate balance. Obsession should be a driving force, not an all-consuming fire. Women who master this art understand that passion should uplift, not overwhelm. Whether pursuing a career, a creative endeavor, or personal growth, the key is to channel obsession positively without sacrificing well-being.

In a world that sometimes misconstrues obsession as a negative force with movies portraying women as stalkers, we can redefine that narrative. We can portray obsession as the unapologetic pursuit of dreams, the drive to overcome obstacles, and the unwavering confidence that transforms our passion into a superpower. So, let's celebrate the women who harness this force, breaking barriers, shattering expectations, and leaving an indelible mark on the world. After all, when obsession meets purpose, incredible things happen, and women step into the fullness of their power.

www.consultkoren.com/ • web.askkoren.app/ • www.linkedin.com/in/koren-norton-08700313/

# SRS ACADEMY
## EMPOWER**HER** HUB

She Rises Studios (SRS) Academy is a groundbreaking online platform exclusive to online educators catering to women entrepreneurs. Our mission is to empower women worldwide through high-level skills courses and workshops that cover a wide range of topics essential for personal growth, career advancement, and business success.

**LEARN MORE**

SheRisesStudios.com/srs-academy

# Trish Rock

## 3 Ways You Can Follow Your Purpose and Passion

If you are feeling like you don't have a purpose, have lost your passion for life or are simply in an energetic and physical void right now you are not alone. You may have been feeling this way for a few years now when our lives all changed.

Don't pack up your toys out of the sandpit you are in just yet! It will all be clear again soon. But you must have faith.

Everyone has a dream, a soul calling of sorts. Whether that be something big that changes the world or a simple dream of being a great parent. Either way, whatever it is you are here for in this life experience impacts everyone and everything.

Often people say to me that they don't know their purpose, they don't know what their passion in life is.

I feel that we all know this from an early age however we can be talked out of it, told we cannot have it, be trained into believing we are not good enough to pursue it or allow ourselves to stay small to please others – also a trained behaviour.

I also believe that not all of these fears that keep us from being all we can be, are from this one lifetime and if you know a little about my work you will know that I believe this moment is happening across all time and space, and as such, all of our parallel lives are affecting each other.

The fears, the triumphs. The blessings and the dangers, along with all the breakthroughs.

So, if you find yourself at this moment feeling like your vision is crashing down, your purpose is no longer calling you and your passion is less than hot, I want to give you 3 ways you can begin to feel aligned again.

By asking yourself these questions and doing the short exercises, the clarity you once had (or never had!) will arise.

1. Why are you here?
This is always a great exercise to revitalise what you love. Take a piece of paper (I find physically writing rather than typing is more therapeutic). Ask yourself this question: What brings me joy? And then list everything that comes to mind!

2. Who or what are your joy thieves? Are there fears within you that say you cannot have this joy in your life? Are there people around you who judge or criticize you for experiencing joy? Are there old beliefs and fears within you that block your every move towards your purpose and joy?

3. What can you do, be, feel, think, act on today that brings you joy and feels purposeful? Could you inspire someone? Could you help someone? Could you create something? Could you give extra hugs to your family? Could you go take a bit of time for yourself somewhere? Could you finally clean that clutter up? Could you start a savings plan?

Some of these things may seem like they have nothing to do with your purpose or passion but believe me, if you can bring yourself into the joy of the moment, rather than the feeling of lack of vision right now, everything will start to make sense again AND you will be in Divine flow again, able to receive not only messages, insights and prompts but new opportunities and abundance.

Finally, I want to ask you this: What if, your purpose was to simply be present, here, now, and experience joy, happiness, and love? Would that be less demanding and self-pressured than all the 'doing' you may have told yourself you need? Give these new perceptions a test run and see for yourself what might happen. I hope you find you are achieving more, have more flow and ease, while stressing less and doing less.

www.trishrock.com • www.linkedin.com/in/TrishRock

# CONSTANTINE FOXX

My name is Constantine. I come from a Greek background, born in Australia. As you may know, we show love through food. Hence, I was never a very overweight girl growing up, but definitely fuller compared to my fabulous Aussie friends. In 2008, I suffered a severe back work injury which left me with bulging discs, and upon further investigation,

I have a Neurofibroma on my spinal nerve, a double whammy. With this injury, my life fell into a downward spiral. I developed type 2 diabetes as I could not exercise or move around like I used to. I developed depression and started to comfort eat. So, between being on insulin five times per day and eating, my weight ballooned to 105 kg. I am 5 ft 1. I had 50% visceral fat around my organs, on my way to an early grave.

I took action. I tried dieting to no avail; nothing worked long term. I said ENOUGH. Something switched in my mind. I found the right surgeon for Bariatric surgery; it was my last attempt.

I started getting my mindset right. WOW, I thought, if I'm going under the knife, I'm doing this correctly. I did my homework. What worked for me was a whole lot of personal purging and believing in myself. I did the surgery.

In six months, I lost 55 kgs. YES!!! I did it, but my journey had just begun. My transformation was fantastic. I also became a Life Coach so I can help other women in similar positions. So, I am now a FOXXY FIERCE & FABULOUS mindset Coach/Mentor.

I have successfully helped high-profile clients in Dubai & Europe. I am here to help anyone. First, we see if we're a good fit, then work out the program, which is as unique as their own fingerprint. I never use the exact same program twice. I help and rejoice in all your triumphs. I live and love to see you succeed and watch the fabulous TRANSFORMATION.

# 7 GOOD HABITS OF A MENTALLY STRONG WOMAN

If you still think that mentally strong women are born, may be right, but I believe you have what it takes to develop strength in your thoughts and habits. Strong women are able to make. It takes effort and you are well- equipt to make the choices that will get you there. It's all about knowing your strengths and flaws, setting intentions to get better every day, and protecting yourself when others try to attack you. You can't become a strong woman by reading a book or attending a workshop – you have to act like one.

*Here are some habits of strong women you should consider adopting:*

## 1. She doesn't compare herself to other women

Measuring what she has in life in terms of people, wealth, and appearance only drains her strength. A strong woman doesn't really care about what others are doing – good or bad. She doesn't see other women as their competition; she only competes with the person she was yesterday.

She doesn't like to see others failing in order to feel like she is winning. In fact, she rejoices for young girls and women when they achieve their goals because it strengthens her belief that she'll also get what she is trying to achieve.

## 2. She refuses to see herself as a victim

No matter how hard things go for them, she doesn't see herself as a victim. It's hard to ditch the victim mentally, especially when women all over the world have been oppressed throughout history and still don't always get an equal place as men in society, repeating it, again and again, will only perpetuate this belief.

Although everyone is a victim of something in life, the label 'victim' only promotes powerlessness. That's why she wants to be seen as a survivor which is a true symbol of empowerment.

## 3. She is honest with herself

She doesn't seek comfort in ignoring the harsh phases of life. While sometimes it is necessary to shut o the memory, a woman who does this constantly lives in a fake paradise. A strong and independent woman isn't afraid to accept both good and bad experiences in her life. In fact, she likes to be brutally honest about herself as it motivates her to improve.

## 4. She doesn't blame herself

Self-blaming is a kind of emotional abuse that ultimately pushes her into a torturous cycle. She stops blaming herself for things she did and things she couldn't do. Being strong means, she accepts the actions for which she holds responsibility, but it doesn't mean that she sees herself at fault for everything that happened to her.

Beautiful people suffering from horrible things. This is life. God says the rain falls on the just and the unjust. Don't try to find the 'absolute or hidden' meaning behind tragedies of the past.

## 5. She doesn't exclusively depend on others

One of the most important factors that differentiate a strong woman from others is that she doesn't rely on others to save her. She knows she possesses all the power to rise above the stormy phases of life. She doesn't wait for others to come and pick her up when things don't go well for her. She is a self-sufficient person and understands that throwing a pity party isn't going to remove all problems in her life. There are times to ask for help. With that said, her power lies in the ability to act in her own best interest.

## 6. She doesn't let society determine her worth

While it can be tempting to allow others to bring you down with rejection and criticism, a strong woman knows that other people don't determine their self-worth. Even if she is surrounded by disapproval or harsh comments from loved ones, that doesn't make her worthless. A mentally strong woman isn't bothered by rude comments. The struggles of life have made her resilient. She leans on her faith that each one of us was born with a purpose, all divinely planned. She develops coping skills that help her bounce back when life gets tough.

## 7. She prepares for the worst

Sure, having a positive mindset that sees the good even in challenging times can be great, but preparation makes life easier. She capitalizes on what comes next in life. Instead of getting stuck because of obstacles, she creates an action plan and deals with them confidently as they appear. She sees obstacles as challenges and sees what opportunities she has in it.

## Written by Julianne Williams

Julianne Williams is an independent woman, a single mother, and a blog writer who rises from depression and hopelessness to the President of a large privately owned company. Her bestselling book 'Head Above Water: A Journey of Emerging Hope' is about nding strength and inner light when life treats us unfairly. The chapters discusses her life struggle being a widow and a single mother but are also packed with inspirational statementsandquotestoalteryourperspective. Sheisalsoco-authorof internationally best-selling books "Unleash Her" and "Mom Magic Mompreneur". She's on a mission to support young women who lost their husbands and trying to navigate the pressure society. This ink-and-paper hug is a reminder for you to never lose hope, work hard, keep your chin up, your chest out, and trust the timing.

🌐 www.juliannewilliams.com
🌐 www.conizo.com/shop
f www.facebook.com/BraveEnoughCommunity
in www.linkedin.com/in/julianne-williams-1aa76917

# NOW AVAILABLE

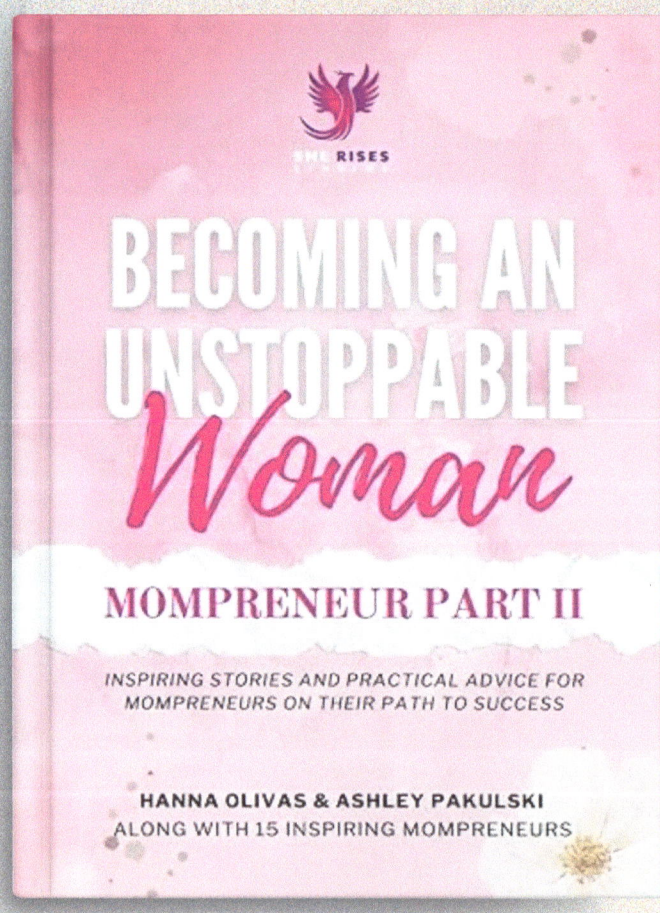

Discover stories of remarkable women
who are both moms and entrepreneurs

WWW.BIT.LY/BAUWMOMPRENEURTWO

# Breaking Free: A Journey from Childhood Trauma to Healing

*Emily Cleghorn*

You're searching for answers— you've googled "how to overcome childhood trauma" more times than you'd like to admit and you've done more therapy than a little but you're not getting the outcomes you're wanting.

**I get it— I've been there too.**

For so much of my life, I believed that I was a waste of space and that no one cared if I was even here. I spent much of my life to this point making myself so small and invisible to not take up any space. I never felt like I fit anywhere I went— even within the biological families I was born into which gave way to a deeply rooted sense of loneliness. Those big scary emotions— the remnants of the trauma— that we've been told for so long are "bad" and shouldn't be expressed are the ones we push down but here's the thing— they come out in some way. Whether it's when your kid is having a temper tantrum and you absolutely lose it or someone isn't going as fast through the checkout at the grocery store and you become irritable and downright mean to anyone within earshot.
Perhaps it isn't just your emotions being dysregulated where your trauma makes itself known. Maybe you also struggle with digestive disorders or hormonal imbalances. This too, is trauma's impact on your body.

What I have come to understand is that trauma doesn't just impact one area of an individual's life but it has a far-reaching and long-lasting impact if we choose to continue to allow it to run our lives. I've also learned that every system and every aspect of our lives— our physical well-being, emotional well-being, spiritual, financial, and relational well-being are all connected. Nothing is isolated.

So, if our trauma was the majority psychological and there were no visible bruises or cuts... that trauma, those words and mind games still have an impact on your physical health. They can still cause physical illness just like being physically beaten up.

There comes a point in your healing journey when you have to stop focusing on the traumatic events and start focusing on breaking free and what has helped you rise up out of the ashes to live life on the other side of the trauma. For those, like me, who have childhood trauma that has impacted us on a developmental level, it's hard to know who we are as individuals without the trauma and that seems like a ridiculous thing to even say because we will never be without the trauma. It will always be there but it doesn't have to rule over our lives. We can break free.

Breaking free from the bondage of trauma is a feat that seems impossible because the trauma and those who traumatized you have led you to believe that life is just a miserable existence and we have no hope of being loved, seen or valued.

I am here to tell you these things couldn't be further from the truth and although healing from a traumatic childhood especially while parenting is one of the most challenging things you can do, it is possible.
Join me on the "Mamahood After Trauma Podcast", where we navigate mamahood while healing childhood trauma. This podcast provides tools and resources, candid discussions and insights to help you find grace and ease in your journey. Remember, healing is possible, and you are worthy of a life free from the shadows of trauma. Let's embark on this journey together towards healing and reclaiming our lives.

home.mendedmamalife.ca • home.mendedmamalife.ca/blog

emily.cleghorn.coach     mamahoodaftertrauma

# FOR SUCH A TIME AS THIS...BE YOU!

## WRITTEN BY: CAROLYN DECK

"Above the Turbulence. Your Ticket Out Of Pain to Purpose" shares my journey and transformation to becoming the best me. My dream and goal is to encourage and inspire others to discover themselves, a call to BE YOU.

The tangled mess living in life's chaos poses the question, "Who am I?" Writing my story, a journey of discovery, I learned the power we all have - CHOICE.

"CHOICE DEFINES...How I respond is the key to my destiny." Carolyn Deck

Understanding the power of your response will take you to a destiny you never thought possible. "Why?" is needed, however, asking '"what?"will drive you on. Gives you choice. Stop and ask; What do you believe, controlling your actions resulting in the outcomes of your life? What lie may be hiding in what you beLIEve? What if you are living a lie believing what someone said about you? Or what you tell yourself. What thoughts do you need to examine to BE YOU?

Through life's reflective lens, I uncovered beauty, even in the chaos. This changed everything. Amid dysfunction, a powerful realization struck: Get Out of Dysfunction, Give Order in the Decision, Greatness Out of Despair - G.O.D. I choose to see, listen, feel and believe Him. He was always there, even when I didn't know Him or feel His presence. He not only loves me tenderly, He knows me better than I know myself.

His light of truth transformed my thinking out of the lens of my wounded experiences and trauma, and I turned off those destructive voices of others and those I listened to in my head. From questioning everything to the embrace of who I am through the eyes of God who made me, obviously not perfect, I am uniquely me. He taught me what He wants for me..."BE YOU."

**FACT: Comparison is a killer.** God created you uniquely to BE YOU. Know this - originals are way more valuable than any copy will ever be. You are beautiful, greatly loved, immeasurably valuable, and fully accepted as you are. No need for comparison or compromise. KNOW YOU. BE YOU.

Striding out, holding His trustworthy hand, I walk with confidence, every next step because I know who and whose I am. Firmly rooted in God's love for me, I travel this world knowing I am passing through with my final home in my sights - Heaven. This truth takes me above the turbulences of life giving me a higher perspective and a greater purpose. I trust in God's boundless understanding and unwavering love. Believing in God's infinite wisdom and unconditional love allows me to surrender my limitations receiving His gifts of strength and guidance, peace and hope. The joy of His resurrection empowers me to embrace all life has for me. I live fully with purpose and gratitude. My book is my testimony and my legacy.

f 🅾 carolyn.deck

# Elevate your brand through creative and impactful content!

# EMPOWER**HER** CONTENT DAY

## SEPTEMBER 21, 2024 | LOS ANGELES, CALIFORNIA

GET YOUR EARLY BIRD TICKET TODAY: $97

WWW.SHERISESSTUDIOS.COM/CONTENT-DAY

EmpowerHer Content Day equips attendees with the tools and knowledge needed to craft compelling content for social media, podcasts, and videos.

# *Alondra* Rena Hubbard

**Alondra Rena creator of The Cozy Conversations.** dxb w/ Alondra Rena Podcast is an American, currently living in Dubai, UAE. Her profession as a professional celebrity makeup artist in film and entertainment has allowed her to work closely with some amazing entrepreneurs, artists, actors, creators, and business owners.

The Cozy Conversations dxb" w/Alondra Rena is a podcast that resonates with many listeners, offering a blend of personal growth, cultural exchange, and professional insights. The international aspect certainly adds a unique touch, reflecting the diverse experiences and viewpoints of its host and guests.

This podcast focuses on cross-cultural experiences or interviews with a diverse range of guests discussing their life journeys and professional endeavors. Exploring different perspectives can be both enlightening and entertaining.

Facebook @alondrarena
Instagram @alondrarena
YouTube @thecozyconversations.dxb w/Alondrarena
tiktok @a.rena2

# Intentionally Leading with Confidence

*By Evangelist Tamala J. Coleman*

## What is the difference between feeling confident and feeling Empowered?

Over the last couple of years I've been endowed with Speaking, Ministering and doing what I love best, Encouraging others, Empowering others with my God-Given Gifts, Talents and anointing.

For me, there is one essential difference between the two: Confidence and Empowerment. If you are confident in yourself as a person no one has to pat you on the back or say "Good Job" . I am confident in who I am and what I do without being self-doubtful or second thinking myself. An empowered person also has confidence and desire to do more and reinvent themselves daily. (to do, change, or improve something).

What does it mean to be empowered? To feel empowered is to be self-aware (to know your strengths and your weaknesses to have self-confidence and believe that you can do anything that you set your mind to do.

It is essential that you have a high degree of self-awareness. For example, you need to know your core values, motivations, strengths, and weaknesses and what your heart desires and your personal goals.

You know you better than anyone. If you don't know these things about yourself, instead of feeling empowered you'll probably feel lost, or disconnected, or frustrated about wanting to make changes to your life but not knowing where to start. You may even feel doubtful of what you can do.

There was a time in my life when I did not feel confident in my decisions to own my own business, but I took the first steps to make my dreams come true and at the same time I am a living testimony to what God can do when you just take the first step to confidence in yourself.

Psychologists and Therapists encourage people to develop their self-awareness because knowing yourself can help you to better manage your thoughts, emotions and behaviors. Ultimately this helps you to have greater success in your relationships and your work.

You may have read hundreds of self-help books, but you are still hungry to know more about yourself, to learn, and try to be the best you that you can be.

No one knows your heart like God. He knows your very Heart desires as the scriptures tell us that If you delight yourself in Him, He will give you the desires of your Heart.( Psalm 37:4).

Iam_TamalaColeman

tamala.coleman.

youtube.com/channel/UCTo6ZtIB7vFOK4oRKiQsTxg

# 6-Figure AUTHOR

Ready to turn your passion for writing into a thriving 6 figure income 🚀

Join the exclusive "6 Figure Author" program and unlock the strategies and support you need for unparalleled success!

**SIGN UP NOW**

**SIGN UP HERE:**
www.sherisesstudios.com/6figureauthor

# Transform Challenges into Opportunities for Growth

*Cynthia Concordia*

**How Come When You Seek Growth You Are Scared of Challenges?**

**According to C.S. Lewis, "Hardships often prepare ordinary people for an extraordinary destiny."**

When you seek growth, it is essential to recognize that challenges are the very soil in which growth takes root. Imagine a seedling pushing through the earth, reaching for the sun. It doesn't shy away from the resistance of the soil; instead, it embraces it. The struggle strengthens its stem, deepens its roots, and propels it toward the light.

Similarly, in our lives, challenges serve as catalysts for transformation. They force us to adapt, learn, and evolve. Without them, growth would be stagnant—a mere illusion.

So, when you encounter challenges, don't be afraid. Lean into them. Embrace the discomfort, for it is the forge where your character is shaped.

Growing because of trials can also be compared to the oyster that has a little piece of sand lodged inside. In response to this intruder, the oyster makes the most of its trial and makes a beautiful pearl! Without the challenge or setback of having this uncomfortable piece of sand, the oyster would never have made the pearl.

When I reached a point in my life that I was at my rock bottom after the death of my husband, I had to go out of my comfort zone so I may be able to work on myself; my relationship with my children, family and friends; my work and my finances.

When I faced my challenges to become the new Cynthia, a lot of opportunities came up and still continue to show up. I never imagined myself doing what I am doing right now, helping and impacting people to be the best version of themselves.

**So how do you transform challenges into opportunities for growth?**

1. Be open. Changing our minds about something can be an extremely liberating act that expands our horizons. Looking at the same issue through a different lens has a way of opening up new doors of possibilities that can actually help us see things from a fresh and hopeful perspective. It becomes more natural to feel compassion for other people and for us. We can come closer to finding the lesson or opportunity for growth in just about any situation.

2. Be honest. What is it that we truly want? How are we really feeling? Putting on a brave face can create the illusion to everyone around us that everything is great, but if we aren't being honest with ourselves, it won't be long before a serious feeling of uneasiness creeps into our being. The closer we bring the image we portray out into the world with our inner truth, the more at peace we will be.

3. Continue Trying. If you make a mistake and view that mistake as helpful, it builds up persistence. If you think "Well, if that didn't work, I'll try it a different way. If you continue to persevere, then that's a sign of you being totally engaged. Good thing is if you persevere in one area, this proof can carry over to other challenges.

4. Learn to effectively deal with emotion. Don't be bitter. Feelings will come; don't hold grudges. Learn to forgive has taught me that there are no boundaries in life. Bitterness is what creates boundaries.

Remember, the path to growth is often paved with obstacles, but each hurdle you overcome adds another layer to your resilience. Keep pushing forward, my friend.

*Cynthia Concordia*
*CEO & Founder*
*Dream to Rise LLC*
*www.dreamtorise.info*

www.dreamtorise.info • FB: cynthia.concordia • LinkedIn: cynthia-concordia-2b51b8116 • IG: cynthiaconcordia

# Spiritually Empowered Horsemanship: Unveiling a Deeper Connection

by: Cindy Hartzell

In a world where connections between hearts and horses can transcend the traditional, "Spiritually Empowered Horsemanship Podcast" emerges as a beacon for those seeking to explore the profound depths of their relationship with equines. Hosted by Cindy and Laura, two horsewomen from vastly different backgrounds, this podcast is a testament to the transformative power of spiritually aligned horsemanship. Their mutual passion for horses goes much deeper than the conventional, nurturing a shared vision that has brought to life a unique platform for empowerment and connection.

## The Genesis of a Vision

Cindy and Laura's journey is nothing short of inspiring. Despite their differing paths in the equestrian world, it was their shared profound experiences and life lessons learned from horses that united them. Together, they realized that the essence of horsemanship extends far beyond the physical realm, into an energetic world that, while invisible, is intensely alive and transformative. This realization was the spark that ignited the creation of the "Spiritually Empowered Horsemanship Podcast."

## A Mission to Empower

At its core, the podcast aims to empower listeners to delve beneath the surface of their horsemanship journey, encouraging them to seek a deeper connection, more meaning, and greater confidence in their equine endeavors. Cindy and Laura believe that there's more to life with horses than the conventional training and daily routines. They advocate for an exploration into the energetic connection between horse and human, a venture that promises to unlock unprecedented potential and transform lives.

## Who Is It For?

"Spiritually Empowered Horsemanship" is a sanctuary for the heart-driven equestrian, whether seasoned or new to the world of horses. It serves as a source of inspiration for those who sense that there's more to their journey with horses than meets the eye. The podcast is a call to those eager to explore the unseen energetic world of horsemanship, offering insights, stories, and practices that pave the way for a deeper, more connected life with equines.

## What to Expect

Listeners are invited to join Cindy and Laura every 2nd and 4th Tuesday of the month for episodes that promise to enrich knowledge, ignite imagination, and deepen awareness. The podcast covers a wide array of topics, including navigating relationships with horses, mindful riding practices, trusting intuition in horse training and husbandry, and embracing the beauty of an imperfect journey. Each episode is a step towards a more profound connection with oneself and one's equine companion, guiding listeners to explore the boundaries of what they thought possible.

## A Journey of Transformation

"Spiritually Empowered Horsemanship" is more than just a podcast; it's a movement towards understanding the true essence of connection with horses. Cindy and Laura's passion and dedication shine through each episode, offering a fresh perspective on horsemanship that is both enlightening and deeply moving. Their message is clear: when you tap into the energetic world shared with horses, you unlock a level of potential that can truly transform your life.

In a world where the bonds we forge with our equine partners can lead us on a journey of spiritual and emotional growth, "Spiritually Empowered Horsemanship Podcast" stands out as a guiding light. It invites listeners to embark on a transformative journey, one that promises not just a deeper connection with horses, but a more enriched, confident, and connected life.

www.buzzsprout.com/2343239/share
fb.com/profile.php?id=61557691663962

# The Power of Yo Four Life: Transforming Your life

*Do you stress, have negative spirals in life, or feel anxious often? There's an opportunity for transformation waiting for you. Picture a life where indecision, self-doubt, and fear no longer hold you back. Imagine having the clarity to pursue your dreams with unwavering belief and the resilience to conquer any obstacle. That's the promise of Yo Four Life.*

There's immense power in embracing decisiveness, belief, awareness, and resilience - four principles that transformed my life. I'm passionate about sharing these insights with others who, like me, once felt overwhelmed by pressure, stress, and anxiety, to help them realize they can achieve the life they desire.

### Decisiveness: The Key to Unlocking Your Potential

Indecision is the thief of opportunity, robbing us of the chance to move forward and grow. Man oh man did I sit so often, frozen by what decision I should make, so I made no decision. One Year I DECIDED NO MORE, by embracing decisiveness, we reclaim our power to shape our destiny.

Decisiveness is not about making the perfect choice but about taking action and moving forward with purpose. When we make decisions confidently, we create momentum in our lives, propelling us towards our goals with clarity and conviction. My decisive chart helps those who fear making the wrong decision to take charge and move towards their destiny.

### Belief: Harnessing the Power of Possibility

Our beliefs shape our reality. We have a lot of negative beliefs about who we are and what we can achieve. Let me tell you just as easy as the negative can happen the positive can happen! But you have to work on the thoughts that you allow in. When we believe in ourselves and our dreams, we unlock a world of possibilities.

The belief in the positive gives us the courage to pursue our passions, even in the face of uncertainty. It drives us forward, empowering us to overcome obstacles and achieve our dreams. By cultivating unwavering belief in ourselves, we tap into our limitless potential and create the life we desire.

### Awareness: The Path to Self-Discovery

Self-awareness is the cornerstone of personal growth. It is the ability to observe our thoughts, feelings, and behaviors without judgment, allowing us to understand ourselves more deeply. Self-awareness helped me realize how hard I was on myself. You can't listen to the negative thoughts your brain is repeating to you, you must talk to yourself like you would your best friend. You would never tell your best friend that she is a terrible person who will never make it in life. So DON'T tell yourself that either.

When we cultivate awareness of what is happening in our brain, we gain insight into our patterns and habits, then we can make conscious choices that align with our values and goals. Awareness frees us from the grip of negative self-talk and self-doubt. Then we can treat ourselves like our bestie and embrace our potential with clarity and confidence.

### Resilience: Handling Hard Better

Life is full of challenges, but it is our resilience that determines our ability to overcome them. Resilience is not about avoiding hardship but about facing it head-on with courage and determination. I never realized how every person will experience challenges but it is all in how they react in these moments. Do they let their emotions take over or do they stop recognize the negative feeling but then respond to what is going on with clarity and courage.

As we cultivate resilience to the emotional response, we bounce back from setbacks stronger and more powerful than before. We learn from our experiences, adapting and growing in the face of adversity. Resilience allows us to navigate life's ups and downs with grace, knowing that we have the strength to overcome any obstacle. There is no easy bus everyone, I promise, it is just learning to handle hard better.

Decisiveness, belief, awareness, and resilience are not just individual qualities; they are interconnected pillars that support our journey towards personal growth and fulfillment. By embracing these four principles, we unlock our true potential and create a life filled with purpose, passion, and possibility.

My desire for everyone to recognize this brought me a podcast, life coaching business and an online course. YOU can embrace the power of decisiveness, belief, awareness, and resilience, and watch as your life transform in ways you never thought possible. REALIZE THE POWER IS WITHIN YOU!

**CONNECT WITH DIONNE**
KICKSTART FREEBIE: WWW.YOADRIENNETALKS.COM/KICK
IG: YOADRIENNETALKS • FB: YOADRIENNETALKS • TIKTOK: @YOADRIENNETALKS

**WRITTEN BY**
ADRIENNE SWANSON

**WEBSITE**
WWW.YOADRIENNETALKS.COM

# TRUE HEALING OCEAN RETREAT

## A Place to Meet Your Soul

*Down to Earth Luxury Among the Mountains, Salish Sea & Rainforest*
*East Sooke, BC, Canada*

### Intimate Solo & 2 Person Retreats

Hosting up to 2 guests at a time for a deep meaningful stay. Customize as you desire!

truehealingoceanretreat.com

**Book Your Stay Today!**

# Embrace Your Reflection: Cultivating a Positive Body Image

**BY: YOLANDA MARTINEZ**

In today's society, where beauty standards are often unattainable and unrealistic, cultivating a positive body image is more important than ever. Our perception of our bodies significantly influences our self-esteem, confidence, and overall well-being. However, embracing and celebrating our unique selves can be a powerful journey toward self-love and acceptance.

Embracing Diversity and Rejecting Unrealistic Standards should be a top priority.

The first step in cultivating a positive body image is to recognize and embrace the diversity of human bodies. Every body is unique, with its shape, size, and features. Instead of striving to conform to society's narrow definition of beauty, we must celebrate the beauty of diversity. Everyone is different and unique; wanting to look like someone else can cause you stress, and that will follow unhealthy eating habits.

Rejecting unrealistic beauty standards perpetuated by the media is crucial. Images of airbrushed models and celebrities create an unattainable ideal that leaves many feeling inadequate or insecure about their bodies. It's essential to remind ourselves that these images are often heavily edited and do not represent reality.

Let's start shifting the Focus from Appearance to Functionality.

One way to cultivate a positive body image is to shift the focus from appearance to functionality. Instead of obsessing over how our bodies look, we can appreciate all the amazing things they can do. Our bodies allow us to move, dance, laugh, and experience the world around us. By focusing on what our bodies can accomplish rather than how they appear, we can develop a deeper sense of appreciation and gratitude for them.

Engaging in physical activities that we enjoy can help us positively connect with our bodies. Whether it's dancing, hiking, swimming, or practicing yoga, finding activities that bring us joy and make us feel strong can boost our self-esteem and body confidence. The key element here is to honor how you feel instead of how you look. If your focus is on feeling good, looking good will also come into play. Daily exercise activity boosts your energy and boosts your self-confidence. These two positive feelings will motivate you to have more feel-good habits.

Always remember that Practicing Self-Compassion and Kindness will boost your self-confidence.

Self-compassion is another essential component of cultivating a positive body image. We must learn to treat ourselves with the same kindness and understanding we would offer a friend. Instead of criticizing ourselves for perceived flaws or imperfections, we can practice self-compassion by speaking to ourselves with gentleness and encouragement.

Challenging negative self-talk is critical to fostering self-compassion. When we catch ourselves engaging in self-criticism, we can replace those negative thoughts with affirmations emphasizing our worth beyond physical appearance. Remembering that we are more than just our bodies – we are intelligent, creative, and capable individuals – this can help us develop a more balanced and compassionate view of ourselves.

Surrounding Ourselves with Positive Influences creates a supportive environment.

The people and media we surround ourselves with can have a significant impact on our body image. Surrounding ourselves with positive influences – friends, family members, and social media accounts that promote body positivity – can help reinforce a healthy and realistic view of beauty.

Seeking out diverse representations of beauty in the media can also be empowering. Following accounts celebrating body diversity and featuring individuals of all shapes, sizes, and backgrounds can help us feel more represented and validated in our unique bodies.

Embracing Your Unique Self

Cultivating a positive body image is a journey that requires patience, self-compassion, and intentionality. By embracing diversity, shifting our focus from appearance to functionality, practicing self-compassion and kindness, and surrounding ourselves with positive influences, we can foster a healthier and more balanced relationship with our bodies.

Remember that your body is worthy of love and appreciation precisely as it is. Embrace your uniqueness, celebrate your strengths, and remember that true beauty comes from within. When you feel good about yourself, it will reflect on the outside in how you treat yourself and others. As we continue cultivating a positive body image, we should also strive to create a world where all bodies are accepted, celebrated, and valued.

www.21dayswithyolanda.com
https://www.instagram.com/iamyolandamartinez/
https://www.facebook.com/yshoegal
https://www.linkedin.com/in/yolanda-martinez-24606913/

# TRANSFORMATIVE BALANCE:
## JENNIFER'S JOURNEY TO PRIORITISING HEALTH AND WEALTH

*Amy Walker*

Before Jennifer decided to prioritise her health and wealth, her life was a chaotic whirlwind. She was always on the go, juggling a demanding job, social commitments, and countless other responsibilities. Amidst the chaos, she neglected her well-being, surviving on convenience foods and caffeine-fueled nights, while her finances remained in disarray, with little thought given to budgeting or saving.

But one day, Jennifer had a revelation. She realised that true happiness and fulfilment couldn't be found in constant busyness and neglect of her own needs. Determined to make a change, she sought the guidance of a coach who could help her navigate the path towards balance and well-being.

Under the coach's guidance, Jennifer began to transform her life. She carved out time for self-care, prioritising exercise, healthy eating, and mindfulness practices. With the coach's support, she gradually established healthier habits, finding joy in nourishing her body and mind.

As Jennifer's physical health improved, so too did her financial situation. With her coach's assistance, she created a budget, tracked her expenses, and set realistic financial goals. She learned to distinguish between needs and wants, curbing impulse spending and prioritising savings for the future.

The changes didn't happen overnight, but Jennifer's dedication and perseverance paid off. Her home became a sanctuary of calm and tranquility, her once-neglected garden now a thriving oasis of greenery. She found renewed energy and vitality, no longer weighed down by the stress and exhaustion of her former lifestyle.

But perhaps the most significant transformation was Jennifer herself. She radiated confidence and self-assurance, no longer defined by external measures of success or validation. She embraced a life of balance and abundance, finding joy in the simple pleasures of everyday living.

Jennifer's journey serves as a powerful reminder of the importance of prioritizing health and wealth. With the guidance of a coach, she was able to overcome her past habits and create a life that was rich in both physical and financial well-being. And while the road was not always easy, the rewards far outweighed the challenges.

So, let Jennifer's story inspire you to take a step back and reevaluate your own priorities. Consider how you can nurture your health and wealth, and don't hesitate to seek support if needed. For in finding balance between the two, you may just discover a life that is truly worth living.

Free Action Plan Call –
https://link.roasmail.com/widget/bookings/w/hactionplan
www.instagram.com/thedietista
www.facebook.com/thedietista

# *Debi* Lynn

**"The Job Interview"**

Once upon a time, in the quirky town of Resilienceville, lived a grieving parent named Alex. Despite facing unimaginable loss, Alex decided to attend a job interview.
As Alex entered the room, the interviewer asked, "Can you handle high-pressure situations?"

Alex chuckled, "Well, I've navigated grief seminars with toddlers throwing tantrums and teens rolling their eyes. I can handle anything!"

The room burst into laughter. The interviewer smiled, "You're hired for your strength and humor!"

And so, Alex continued helping others find resilience, turning grief into growth.
If you're facing tough times, remember, humor can be your greatest ally. Let's turn challenges into triumphs together!

Join us at <u>Resilienceville.com</u> and let resilience guide your journey.